Edward Badeley

The privilege of religious confessions in English courts of justice considered in a letter to a friend

Edward Badeley

The privilege of religious confessions in English courts of justice considered in a letter to a friend

ISBN/EAN: 9783744715232

Printed in Europe, USA, Canada, Australia, Japan

Cover: Foto ©Lupo / pixelio.de

More available books at **www.hansebooks.com**

THE

PRIVILEGE

OF

Religious Confessions

IN

ENGLISH COURTS OF JUSTICE

CONSIDERED,

IN A LETTER TO A FRIEND.

BY

EDWARD BADELEY, Esq., M.A.,

BARRISTER AT LAW.

LONDON:

BUTTERWORTHS, 7, FLEET STREET,

Late Publishers to the Queen's most excellent Majesty.

HODGES & SMITH, GRAFTON STREET, DUBLIN.

1865.

My dear Sir,

As the question whether a Catholic Priest, or a Protestant Clergyman, may refuse to give evidence in a Court of Justice, respecting matters which have been revealed to him in a religious confession, has lately been raised in Parliament, and elsewhere, I think it right to state my reasons for the opinion which I gave you some time ago, that he may and ought to do so. I feel most sensibly the disadvantages under which I must fulfil my task, after the strong declarations of the Lord Chancellor and Lord Chelmsford, made on the 13th of May last, in the House of Lords, in answer to a question put by Lord Westmeath, at variance with my opinion. There is no person who entertains more sincere respect than I do for those noble and learned Lords, or who receives with greater deference any proposition of law which either of them may enunciate; but as their declarations, on the occasion to which I refer, were not made judicially, nor supported by any legal reasoning, I trust that I shall not be deemed guilty of presumption, if, upon a subject which I have frequently considered, I venture to differ from what they have laid down, and to maintain the view which I have deliberately taken.

In dealing then with this subject, I propose, in the first place, to ascertain what was the rule of the Common Law, prior to that series of events which is commonly called the Reformation; next, to see whether that rule was abrogated or altered, at or after that period; and, lastly, to examine the doctrine laid down by the English writers on evidence, and the authorities upon which they rely.

First, then, with respect to the ancient rule of the Common Law upon this point; and, in order to ascertain it, we must of course consider what was then the rule of the Church upon the subject of Confession; for I think that no laboured argument is needed to prove, that when the State was in strict alliance with the Church, and the Church and the State were both Catholic, the rule of the Church upon any Religious Rite, any matter of religious observance and discipline, which was deemed of universal and absolute obligation, was binding also upon the State, as a body composed of Catholics; and, at all events, that the civil power would not, in any of its departments, except under very special and extraordinary circumstances, act otherwise than in strict accordance with it. We know that such was the case, not only in matters relating to public worship and ecclesiastical ceremonies, but also in those relating to Marriage and Divorce, to Excommunication, to Holy Orders, to the disposal of personal property by Will, and to Intestacy, to the observance of Festivals and Religious Seasons, and to other things which it is needless to enumerate. Even many of our old legal maxims are evidently derived from the Canon Law. It would be irrational therefore to doubt, that in a matter of so serious and so general concern, so important and so imperative, as the Sacrament of Penance, all that the Church enjoined with regard to its due administration, to the conduct, and the protection, of those who administered or received it, was regarded everywhere as sacred and inviolable.

Let us see then what the Church prescribed respecting the Seal of Confession; and in tracing this historically from the earliest ages of Christianity, I cannot do better than refer to the very learned work of Morinus, " Commentarius His-" toricus de Disciplinâ in administratione Sacra-" menti Pœnitentiœ," published at Antwerp in the year 1682. In the 19th Chapter of the Second Book, which is entitled, " Confessionis sigillum " nunquam esse resignandum ab Apostolis continuâ " traditione accepit Ecclesia," he begins by saying,

" Nonnulla nobis obiter dicta sunt quæ ad confes-
" sionis sigillum spectare possunt; verum hoc capite
" illius non resignandi necessitatem ex Antiquorum
" testimoniis demonstrare proponimus. Lectoris
" enim scire interest nihil nunc ab Ecclesiâ de isto
" sigillo doceri, quod ab antiquâ traditione non
" acceperit." He then proceeds to adduce the testimony of the principal of the early Fathers, both of
the Eastern and the Western Church, and the
Canons of various Councils, both Greek and Latin,
to that effect; and he concludes by citing the 21st
Canon of the 4th Council of Lateran, (a general
Council, whose decrees were binding on all the
Churches of Christendom, held in the year 1215,
under Pope Innocent III.,) which he calls " Canon
" notissimus," and which he gives in these words;
" Caveat autem omnino sacerdos, ne verbo, aut
" signo, aut alio quovis modo aliquatenus prodat
" peccatorem. Sed si prudentiori consilio indigu-
" erit, illud absque ullâ expressione personæ cautè
" requirat. Quoniam qui peccatum in pœnitentiali
" judicio sibi detectum præsumpserit revelare, non
" solum a sacerdotali officio deponendum decer-
" nimus, verum etiam ad agendam perpetuam
" Pœnitentiam in arctum Monasterium detru-
" dendum." He adds, as his general inference
from the authorities which he has adduced, " Ex
" iis quæ dicta sunt manifestum puto, nihil nunc

" in Ecclesiâ doceri de confessionis sigillo, ŋişi quod
" ab Apostolicâ traditione accepit."

When therefore Gratian first reduced the Canon
Law into method, by the publication of the " Decretum," about the year 1151, it is evident, that, in
stating the Law respecting the sacredness and inviolability of confession, he stated only the Law of
the universal Church, derived from the earliest ages;
the punishment to be inflicted on the Priest who
violated it may have differed at different periods,
but the Law was undoubtedly the same, and had
been sanctioned by penalties similar to those im-
posed by the " Decretum." The passage in the
" Decretum" occurs under the title " De Pœni-
" tentiâ,"* and is as follows :—

" Deponatur sacerdos qui peccata pœnitentis pub-
" licare præsumit."

" Sacerdos ante omnia caveat, ne de his qui ei
" confitentur peccata alicui recitet, non propinquis,
" non extraneis, neque, quod absit, pro aliquo
" scandalo. Nam si hoc fecerit, deponatur, et
" omnibus diebus vitæ suæ ignominiosus peregri-
" nando pergat."

In the Decretals, the next portion of the Canon
Law, the Law is stated to the same effect; for under
the title, " De Pœnitentiis et Remissionibus, tit. 38,
c. xii," the same Canon of the Council of Lateran

* Decreti secunda Pars – Distinct. vi. c. 2.

is set forth, which I have already given in the reference which I have made to Morinus De Pœnitentiâ, and by which a more severe punishment is inflicted, than that which was prescribed in the " Decretum."

Such being the rule of the Canon Law, there could be no reasonable doubt, even if we had not positive evidence of the fact, that it was adopted and enforced in England; but we need not resort to presumptions, for we have, in the Laws of King Henry I., the clearest and most indisputable proof, that this rule of the Church was actually part of the Law of England. Among these Laws we find this, which is remarkable, as being, not only to the same effect, but almost in the same words, as the passage of the " Decretum" which I have cited; " Caveat sacerdos, ne de hiis qui ei confitentur " peccata sua alicui recitet quod ei confessus est; " non propinquis, non extraneis; quod si fecerit, " deponatur, et omnibus diebus vitæ suæ igno- " miniosus peregrinando pœniteat."*

I cite this from the " Ancient Laws and Institutes " of England," published under the authority of " the Commissioners of the Public Records of the " Kingdom," in the year 1840. It is also given in

---

* Leges Hen. primi, v. 17. Ancient Laws and Institutes of England, vol. i. p. 508. Lambard de priscis Anglor. Legibus, p. 178.

the Edition of Lambard's "Archaionomia," published in the year 1644, and in other Treatises
upon our ancient Laws; it is to be found also in
copies of these Laws which exist in manuscript,
not only amongst the ancient Records of the
Realm, but also in private Repositories; so that
there cannot be any doubt of its genuineness
or authenticity. Lord Hale, in the 7th Chapter
of his History of the Common Law, refers to
this Collection of the Laws of Henry I. and cites
it as of considerable authority and value; he says,
" the great essay he (King Henry I.) made was
" the composing of an abstract or manual of Laws,
" wherein he confirmed the Laws of Edward the
" Confessor, 'cum illis emendationibus quibus eam
" 'pater meus emendavit Baronum suorum con-
" 'cilio,' and then adds his own laws, some whereof
" seem to taste of the Canon Law. The whole
" Collection is transcribed in the Red Book of the
" Exchequer, from whence it is now printed in the
" end of Lambard's Saxon Laws, and therefore not
" needful to be here repeated;"—and, after quoting
some passages in confirmation of certain statements
which he had himself made, Lord Hale adds,
" These Laws of King Henry I. are a kind of
" miscellany, made up of those ancient Laws,
" called the Laws of the Confessor, and King
" William I., and of certain parts of the Canon

" and Civil Law, and of other provisions, that
" custom, and the prudence of the King and
" Council, had thought upon, chosen, and put
" together." Lord Coke likewise refers to them
as one of the sources, and as evidence, of the Common Law.*

Now as Henry I. began his reign in the year
1100, and died in the year 1135, this Law, establishing the sacredness and inviolability of confession,
thus appears to have prevailed in this country long
before the publication of the " Decretum ;" and
therefore still longer before the Council of Lateran
to which I have referred. Probably it was incorporated with the Laws of Henry I. as well as with
the compilation of Gratian, from the same source,
some well-known General Council, or decree of the
Holy See, then extant in nearly the same form, and
recognized as universally binding;—at all events, we
find it actually part of the Law of England in the
time of King Henry I., and it exists there without
any exception or limitation ; no crimes or sins are
mentioned to which it is not to apply, nor any
tribunal, or place, or proceedings, in which it is not
to be binding.

I may also observe, that in the same volume of
the " Ancient Laws and Institutes of England,"
there are the Laws of King Ethelred, who died in
1016, amongst which I find one in these words, as

Coke's Reps., Pref. to 8th Part.

9

translated from the Saxon : " And let every Chris-
" tian man do as is needful to him; let him strictly
" keep his Christianity, *and accustom himself fre-*
" *quently to shrift, and fearlessly declare his sins,*
" and earnestly pray as he may be instructed ;"*
on which it may fairly be asked, how any " Chris-
" tian man" could "*fearlessly declare his sins*" in
confession, as required by this Law, if he was liable
at the same time to have them divulged by the
Priest ?

The Canon of the Council of Lateran of the year
1215, which I have noted, as guarding the sacredness and inviolability of confession by more severe
penalties than the " Decretum," seems to have been
received immediately in this country, as it is commented upon by one of our earliest Canonists,
John de Athon, who flourished towards the end of
the same century, about the year 1290; and in one
of his notes to the Constitutions of Otho,† referring
to the reluctance of some persons to confess their
sins to the confessor appointed for them, he says,
" Licet timere non oporteret, cum in foro Pœni-
" tentiali confessionem audit sacerdos vice Dei, nec
" prodere potest peccatorem impune. (Extra. de pec.
" et remiss. omnis. § fi.)"

* Ancient Laws and Inst. of England, vol. i. pp. 311, 323.
† See Constitut. Othon. et Othobon., with the Commentary
of John de Athon, p. 15, Oxon. 1679, at the end of Lyndwood's
Provinciale.

But, long before the time of John de Athon, the
Law of the English Church was clear, for in the
Council of Durham, of the year 1220,* I find this
Canon, "Ne Sacerdos revelet Confessionem.—Nullus
" irâ, vel odio, vel Ecclesiæ metu, vel mortis, in
" aliquo audeat revelare confessiones, signo, vel
" verbo, generali vel speciali, ut dicendo, ' Ego
" ' scio quales vos estis,' sub periculo Ordinis et
" Beneficii, et si convictus fuerit, absque miseri-
" cordiâ degradabitur." A Canon, in almost the
very same words, appears in the previous Constitutions of Richard Bishop of Sarum, of the year
1217.† And in the Provincial Council of Oxford,
held under Archbishop Langton in the year 1222,‡
it was enacted, " Nullus sacerdos, irâ, aut metu
" etiam mortis, audeat detegere confessionem ali-
" cujus, signo, vel verbo, generaliter aut specialiter,
" et si super hoc convictus fuerit, sine spe relaxa-
" tionis non immerito debet degradari." The same
law appears also in the acts of the Synod of Exeter,
held in the year 1287.§

The authority next in order of time, to which I
must direct your attention, is the Statute passed
in the 9th year of Edward II. (A.D. 1315), stat. 1,
called " Articuli Cleri," c. 10—a Statute on which

* Wilk. Conc. vol. i. p. 577.
† Spelm. Conc. vol. ii. p. 145.
‡ Wilk. Conc. vol. i. p. 595.
§ Spelm. Conc. vol. ii. p. 357.

Lord Coke has largely commented in his Second Institute, p. 599—638. It is of value to my present purpose, as evidence of the connexion of the Law of the Church with the Law of the State, on the subject of Confession, in the judgment of no less a person than Lord Coke, at least in all cases below the crime of Treason. Whether he was justified in making that exception, I shall consider presently. The 10th chapter of the Statute relates to the cases of persons claiming the privilege of sanctuary, and abjuring the realm, whose rights, it was alleged, had been violated; to which the answer given is this; " Qui terram abjuraverint, dum sint in Stratâ " publicâ, sunt in pace Domini Regis, nec debent " ab aliquo molestari; et dum sint in Ecclesiâ, " custodes eorum non debent morari infra cœmi- " terium, nisi necessitas, vel evasionis periculum, " hoc requirat; nec arctentur confugere dum sint " in Ecclesiâ, quin possint habere vitæ necessaria, " et exire libere pro obsceno pondere deponendo. " Placet etiam Domino Regi, ut latrones vel ap- " pellatores quandocunque voluerint possint sacer- " dotibus sua facinora confiteri; sed caveant con " fessores, ne erronice hujusmodi appellatores in- " forment." There are some verbal discrepancies between the passage thus given by Lord Coke, and the corresponding ones, as they appear in Ruffhead's edition of the Statutes, vol. 1, p. 169, and

in the more valuable and important work called
" The Statutes of the Realm," published by the
authority of the Crown in the year 1810—vol. 1,
p. 172—but these discrepancies do not materially
affect the sense, and may be disregarded. What
is material is, that the right of Confession to a
Priest is distinctly and in terms secured to the
criminals to whom the Statute relates, and that
this right carried with it, in the judgment of Lord
Coke, a common law right to the privilege of concealment. Lord Coke's commentary is as follows:—
" Latrones vel Appellatores:—This branch ex-
" tendeth only to thieves and approvers indicted
" of felony, but extended not to high treason; for
" if high treason be discovered to the Confessor,
" he ought to discover it, for the danger that
" thereupon dependeth to the King and the whole
" realm; therefore this branch declareth the com-
" mon law, that the privilege of confession ex-
" tendeth only to felonies; and albeit if a man
" indicted of felony becometh an approver, he is
" sworn to discover all treasons and felonies, yet is
" he not in degree of an approver in law, but only
" of the offence whereof he is indicted; and for
" the rest, it is for the benefit of the King, to move
" him to mercy: so as this branch beginneth with
" thieves, extendeth only to approvers of thievery
" or felony, and not to appeals of treason; for by

" the Common Law, a man indicted of high treason
" could not have the benefit of Clergy (as it was
" holden in the King's time, when this act was
" made), nor any clergyman privilege of confession
" to conceal high treason: and so it was resolved
" in 7 Hen. 5, whereupon Friar John Randolf, the
" Queen Dowager's Confessor, accused her of treason,
" for compassing the death of the King: and so it
" was resolved in the case of Henry Garnet, Supe-
" rior of the Jesuits in England, who would have
" shadowed his treason under the privilege of Confes-
" sion, although in deed he was not only consenting,
" but abetting the principal conspirators of the
" powder treason, as by the record of his attainder
" appeareth; and albeit this act extendeth to felo-
" nies only, as hath been said, yet the caveat given
" to the confessors is observable, *ne erronice in-*
" *forment.*"

Now, in examining this Commentary, I must confess, that if Lord Coke really meant to say, *that the
Statute in question gave the Seal of Confession* to the
criminals whom it mentioned, he was, in my opinion,
mistaken. The Statute merely provided, that
" Thieves and Approvers" should be allowed the
benefit of confessing their sins to their Priests
whenever they wished; but of the secrecy of their
confessions it said nothing—for the " Caveat" at
the end of the passage, whatever be its true mean-

ing, (and it is capable of several interpretations) can scarcely be construed to mean this:—Lord Coke may fairly be understood to have intended, (and this explanation protects alike his latin and his legal learning,) that the Statute, by establishing the right of these criminals to go to their Confessors, established also their right to the Seal of Confession, as a right annexed to Confession by the Common as well as by the Ecclesiastical Law; for Lord Coke must have known full well, as everybody knows who has the least acquaintance with the subject, that the Seal or Secrecy of Confession was implied in the very existence of the Rite itself; that a Priest, by administering the Sacrament of Penance, bound himself by his very act to secrecy,—a secrecy which he could not violate without mortal sin, and the forfeiture of all that was most valuable in life. He is therefore quite right in saying, that the Common Law and the Statute give the privilege of Confession to felonies, and therefore, of course, to minor offences; but when he also says, that "this branch "of the Statute declareth that the privilege of "Confession extendeth *only* to Felonies," he evidently states what is untrue—for the Statute "declareth" no such thing—it says nothing whatever about treason or traitors;—nor does it, in fact, about misdemeanors, and yet Lord Coke, upon his own principle of construction, could not deny that the privilege extended to them;-- but in saying that " this branch extendeth not to High Treason," and forming *therefrom* an argument that traitors were not entitled to the privilege of having their confessions concealed, he was neither legally nor logically right; for although it is undoubtedly true, that when a Statute treats of things or persons of an inferior description, it cannot be extended to include those of a superior, (and of that rule Lord Coke was most fully aware,) the consequence of course is, that the superior things and persons are in no way affected; and therefore the confessions of traitors are necessarily left, so far as this Statute is concerned, in precisely the same situation that they were in before. If then the Statute does not in any way relate to Traitors, we must look to the Common Law, to see if there was any difference between their confessions, and those of Felons and others. But neither the Common Law nor the Ecclesiastical, so far as I have been able to discover, recognises any distinction of the sort. The Law of Henry I. cited above, applies, as we have seen, to *all* Confessions, whosesoever they are, and so do the Laws of the Church which I have already quoted, as well as those which I shall quote presently; and Lord Coke's Law, as well as his Logic, must be deemed in this respect equally faulty, unless some very clear authority can be brought to support him,—

for the presumption undoubtedly is strongly against him. Now he does cite two cases, as proof " that " no Clergyman had by the Common Law any " privilege of Confession to conceal High Treason ;" for he says, " so it was resolved in 7 Hen. 5, " whereupon Friar John Randolf, the Queen " Dowager's Confessor, accused her of treason, for " compassing the death of the King ; and so it was " resolved in the case of Henry Garnet, Superior of " the Jesuits in England, who would have sha- " dowed his treason under the privilege of Confes- " sion," &c.

Now it is remarkable, that these two authorities (and he has no other) completely fail him. The case of Friar Randolf has nothing whatever to do with this question. In the first place, nothing is stated in the Rolls of Parliament, to which alone Lord Coke refers, to show that Friar John Randolf was " the Queen Dowager's Confessor," for he is merely described "un frere John Randolf, de " l'ordre des Freres Menours,"* a description which does not involve his being confessor to any- body. In the second place, there is nothing which tends, directly or indirectly, to the belief, that he made any statement of any thing which he had heard in confession, or that he ever was called upon to do so ; in the third place, there is not the slightest trace of any "resolution" of any Court,

* Rot. Parl. vol. iv. p. 118.

or other authority, high or low, upon this subject. Lord Coke cannot possibly have looked at the authority which he cites, or he could not so completely have falsified it. The Record is simply a direction for the Treasurer of England, or his Deputy, to receive and keep all the goods and chattels, and all the lands, rents, tenements, and possessions, of the Queen Dowager, and of two other persons her accomplices, the Queen having been charged on an Information, " tant per relation et confession " d'un frere John Randolf, de 'l'ordre des Freres " Menours, come per autres evidences créables," with having compassed and designed the Death of the King. The Record then directs, that the Treasurer, or his Deputy, shall allow what may suffice for the maintenance of the Queen and her servants, and that those persons who are chargeable with payments to Her Majesty shall be acquitted by payments to the Treasurer, or his Deputy, by force of that ordinance. It seems therefore, that Friar John Randolf was himself an accomplice, and that his own confession of joint criminality was used as evidence against the Queen. The only other particular notices of this man that I have found are in the 3rd Volume of Holinshed's Chronicles, page 106, and in Stow's Annals, page 358, from either of which Lord Coke may possibly have made his statement, that he was the Queen's Confessor; for Holinshed and Stow both say that he had been ; and they state, that he was taken prisoner in Guernsey or Jersey, about the time when the Queen was arrested, that he was thence sent to Normandy, and then by the King's command brought to England, and committed to the Tower, where he was subsequently killed by accident. Holinshed adds, " It was reported that " he had conspired with the Queen by sorcery and " necromancy to destroy the King ;" and Stow says, " that she had devised the King's Death, by the counsel of Randolf;" thus confirming my suggestion, that he was charged as an accomplice in the treason itself, and not examined as a witness : but neither Holinshed, nor Stow, alludes in any way to his having divulged anything which he had heard in confession, or to his having ever been required to do so.

The second of Lord Coke's authorities is no better than the first. It was not " so resolved," as he states, " in the case of Henry Garnet;" there is no trace of any such resolution either in the report of Garnet's trial, which is given in the 2nd Volume of Howell's State Trials, page 217, &c., or in the very careful and able examination and review of the proceedings against him, published by Mr. Jardine in the year 1857, and entitled " A Narrative of the " Gunpowder Plot." Lord Coke, who, as Attorney-General, conducted the prosecution of Garnet, seems to have stated something to the same effect as his commentary on the " Articuli Cleri," but he did so without referring to a single authority, and without the least countenance from the Judges, and therefore his simple " dictum," as Counsel, of what he called the Common Law, is of course of no value. Even if it had been " so resolved " in Garnet's case, as he alleges, the resolution would not have been entitled to much weight, the whole proceedings, including the manner in which Garnet was treated, before, and at, and after his trial, and the Speeches of the Attorney-General Coke, being a disgrace to English Jurisprudence. But the case by no means supports Lord Coke's assertion, that the Common Law disallowed the Seal of Confession in cases of treason ; and it must be remembered moreover that Garnet was not a witness, but a prisoner indicted for Treason, and therefore there could not well be any " resolu- " tion " of the Court, as to his liability to reveal anything which he had heard in confession.

It may seem strange to many persons, that Lord Coke should have made such statements as these ; but every Lawyer, familiar with his writings, well knows, how unscrupulous he was in many respects, and particularly in his references to old cases—a failing which was noticed by Lord Mansfield in the case of The King and Cowle* where he says, " Lord

* 2 Burr. Rep. 859.

c 2

" Coke was very fond of multiplying Precedents and
" authorities, and, in order to illustrate his subject,
" was apt, besides such authorities as were strictly
" applicable, to cite other cases which were not appli-
" cable to the particular question under his judicial
" consideration." And in a much later case* Mr.
Justice Heath remarks, " After all, what reliance can
" there be had on these dicta of Lord Coke, under all
" the circumstances attending them? They were not
" the result of a calm, dispassionate enquiry : that
" great Lawyer was much heated in the controversy
" between the Courts at Westminster and the Eccle-
" siastical Courts. In every part of his conduct his
" passions influenced his judgment. ' Vir acer et
" ' vehemens.' His law was continually warped by
" the different situations in which he found him-
" self." It will not then be an unfair corollary to
say, that in a matter like Confession, to which he
was evidently unfriendly, whatever he admits of its
privilege by the Common Law may safely be received, and what he denies may be rejected, at least
when he adduces no better authorities than those of
Friar John Randolf's Case and Henry Garnet's.

To return however from this digression, and to
proceed in chronological order from the Statute of
Edward II. in the year 1315, when we see, according
to Lord Coke's opinion, that by this statute, and by

* Jefferson v. Bishop of Durham, 1 Bos. & Pull. 131.

the Common Law, Confessions to a Priest, in crimes
below the degree of treason, could not be required in
Evidence.—A Provincial Council, held in England
in the year 1322, passed a Canon in these words:
" Item nullus sacerdos, irâ, odio, vel metu etiam
" mortis, audeat in aliquo detegere alicujus confes-
" sionem, signo vel verbo, specialiter vel generali-
" ter ;—et si super hoc convictus fuerit, sine spe re-
" conciliationis non immerito debet degradari :"—a
canon almost verbatim the same as that passed in
the Council of Oxford, just a century before, which
I have already cited.

At the close of the same century, about the year
1385, we have the celebrated work of John de
Burgh, called the " Pupilla Oculi," a manual composed for the use of the English Clergy, and well
entitled to the great popularity which it is known
to have enjoyed. The author was a writer of considerable authority, for he was Chancellor of the
University of Cambridge, as well as Professor of
Theology, and Rector of Collingham. He therefore
well knew what was the Law universally received in
England upon the subject of Confession ; and of it's
inviolable secrecy he says, " De celatione confessionis
" sciendum est, quod in omni casu tenetur confessor
" celare confessionem sibi factam ; quia sicut Deus
" tegit peccatum interius, ita etiam debet Confessor;
" —et ideo tanquam violator sacramenti peccat, qui

" Confessionem revelat;—unde si aliquod grave peri-
" culum immineret, ut de hæretico qui corrumperet
" fidem, vel de aliquo matrimonio illicito, quod
" aliqui velint contrahere, vel de aliquo magno
" damno temporali, et hoc sciret solum per confes-
" sionem, non debet confessor hoc revelare ; sed
" potius debet eos monere qui confitentur, ut obvient
" vel ut desistant ; et Prælato potest dicere quod
" vigilet super gregem suum, vel aliud simile ; sed
" confitentem nullo modo prodere licet;—nec tenetur
" ad præceptum Prælati revelare aliquid de sibi
" confessis, nec excommunicatio propter hoc in eum
" lata tenet; *nec in testem adductus tenetur aliquid*
" *de his dicere.*"* He then goes on to show, how,
if a Judge should press him upon any matter which
he has only heard in confession, he may answer that
he knows nothing about it, or that he knows nothing
which ought to be disclosed—" *nihil inde scio tibi*
" *revelandum;*"— and he marks the distinctions
very clearly, between what is to be considered as
strictly made known to the Priest in confession, and
what is not. He never suggests the possibility of
the Priest's being committed to prison for his contu-
macy, or of his declining to answer being deemed a
contempt of the Court, or of the Judge's being dis-
satisfied with such a refusal to answer, and it is in
the highest degree improbable, that if any such

* Pupil. Oc. pars quint. cap. 6.

occurrence had been likely to arise, John de Burgh
would not have alluded to it.

The language of Lyndwood,* our greatest canon-
ist, who flourished in the 15th century, and died
A.D. 1446, is to the like effect as that of John de
Burgh, and his comments upon the Provincial
Constitutions which I have cited are so very much
the same, that it would be a needless repetition
were I to extract them at length. It is, however,
material to observe, that neither the one nor the
other makes any such distinction as Lord Coke
suggests, but both agree that the inviolable secrecy
of Confession applies alike to all cases, without exception.

And thus matters continued, till the time of Henry
VIII., without any doubt or question whatever, respecting either the sacredness or the inviolability of
Confession. In fact, these were too well established
to be the subjects of discussion in any of the Courts
of Law, as the whole realm was Catholic, the established Religion was Catholic, and many of the
Judges, from time to time, had been, as Lord Coke
has repeatedly told us, not only Catholics, but Clergymen.† Even therefore if we had not had the evidence which we have, no reasonable person could
have doubted that the rule which prevailed univer-

* Lynd. Provinc., pp. 334, 335. Ed. Oxon.
† See 1st Inst. 304, b. ; 2nd Inst. 265.

sally elsewhere, from the earliest ages, prevailed also in England :—For otherwise England would have stood alone in Christendom, upon a matter of religion, justly deemed of the very highest importance, and of general obligation and almost daily practice. In such a case, the very silence of authors is no slight evidence ; for in an age when Treasons were common, and other capital Felonies very numerous, cases bearing upon this subject must often have arisen. But although we meet with many instances, in the old books, of confessions obtained by various means, there are none, so far as I can discover, relating to confessions of a strictly religious character, nor can I find any case recorded, in which a Priest was required to give evidence of anything which he had heard in the confessional.

And if the privilege of confession was thus secured by the common law, and parcel of that law, as I confidently maintain that it was, I would fain ask, whether up to this period, any Act of Parliament had altered or infringed it ? for I certainly am at a loss to know, how any authority less than that of an Act of Parliament could in any way affect it. Lord Coke says,* " the common law " has no controller in any part of it, but the High " Court of Parliament ; and if it be not abrogated

* 1st Inst. 115, b.

" or altered by Parliament, it remains still, as
" Littelton saith." And Lord Hale declares, to
the same effect,* " this common law, though the
" usage, practice, and decisions, of the King's
" Courts of Justice may expound and evidence it,
" and be of great use to illustrate and explain it,
" yet it cannot be authoritatively altered or changed
" but by Act of Parliament." He then goes on to
explain that many parts of the Canon Law, as well
as of the Civil, have become incorporated with and
parcel of the Common Law of England, and are
therefore unalterable, except by Parliament.

Then was any change made in the reign of
Henry VIII. ? So far from it, a Statute was
passed, the Statute 25 Hen. 8, c. 19, which tends
very strongly to confirm the Law upon the subject of Confession; for in that Statute, by which
the King was authorized to appoint thirty-two
persons to revise the canons, constitutions, and ordinances, theretofore made by the Clergy of the
Realm, there is this proviso, " Provided also, that
" such canons, constitutions, ordinances, and
" synodals provincial, being already made, which
" be not contrariant or repugnant to the laws,
" statutes and customs of this Realm, nor to the
" damage or hurt of the King's Prerogative Royal,
" shall now still be used and executed, as they were

* Hale's Hist. of the Com. Law, Chap. 2.

" afore the making of this Act, till such time as
" they be viewed, searched, or otherwise ordered and
" determined, by the said thirty-two persons, or the
" more part of them, according to the tenor, form
" and effect of this present Act."*

Now the Canons, Constitutions, &c., to which
this Statute refers, undoubtedly comprised those
Provincial Canons and Constitutions respecting
Confession, and the secrecy of Confession in all
cases, to which I have above referred, for they were
certainly in full force, " in viridi observantiâ," at
that time ; and it is clear that the exception in this
Proviso was not intended to exclude them, as, independently of the fact that they were "not con-
" trariant or repugnant to the laws, statutes, and
" customs of this Realm, nor to the damage or
" hurt of the King's Prerogative Royal," the
Statute which was passed some years afterwards,
entitled " An Act abolishing Diversity in Opinions"
(Stat. 31 Hen. 8, c. 14), distinctly and in terms
declared, that " auricular confession was expedient
" and necessary to be retained, and continued, used,
" and frequented, in the Church of God," and that
" Act professes to have been made " by the assent
" of the Lords Spiritual and Temporal, and other
" learned men of the Clergy in Convocation, and
" by the consent of the Commons in Parliament

* See Caudrey's Case, 5 Co. Rep. 32 b.

" assembled, after a great, and long, deliberate, and
" advised disputation and consultation."*

We have thus these Provincial Canons and Constitutions confirmed by an Act of Parliament which
is still in force, for the Stat. 25 Hen. 8, c. 19, though
repealed by the Stat. 1 & 2 Phil. & M. c. 8, was
revived by the Stat. 1 Eliz. c. 1, s. 6, and has remained so to this very day; and we know that the
thirty-two commissioners, appointed by the Crown,
never completed their work. And if those Provincial Canons and Constitutions stand so confirmed, being in strict accordance with the ancient
Common Law, and not abrogated by subsequent
enactments, I must ask those who say, that the
Seal of Confession exists no longer, how they can
support their assertion? No doubt, many of the
ancient Canons and Constitutions to which the
Stat. 25 Hen. 8, c. 19, applies, have lost their
force, in consequence of their incompatibility with
subsequent enactments; but it is for persons who
allege, that those which secure the sacred inviolability of Confession are of this number, to prove
their point by incontrovertible arguments, not by
vague surmises, nor by loose statements of text
writers, nor by *extrajudicial dicta* of Judges, however eminent, or however respected.

Let us see then what happened in the reign of

* See The Statutes of the Realm, Vol. 3, p. 739.

Edward VI., and in the subsequent periods of the Reformation. And here we are at once met by an article in the Royal Injunctions, issued by Edward VI. in the year 1547, directing all " Parsons, " Vicars and other Curates," that " they shall in Confessions every Lent examine *every person* ' *that cometh to Confession to them ;*" &c.* It is evident therefore that the practice of Confession was then not only fully sanctioned, but universally prevalent. In the next year, 1548, the first order for the administration of the Holy Communion was published by the King's authority, and prefaced by a royal proclamation ; and in the Notice, or " Warning," required to be given by the Minister to the Congregation, in the week previous to the Administration of the Sacrament, there occurs this remarkable passage : " And if there be any of you, whose " conscience is troubled and grieved in any thing, " lacking comfort or counsel, let him come to me, or " to some other discreet and learned Priest, taught " in the law of God, and confess and open his sin " and grief secretly, that he may receive such ghostly " counsel, advice, and comfort, that his conscience " may be relieved, and that of us, as a Minister of " God and of the Church, he may receive comfort " and absolution, to the satisfaction of his mind, and " avoiding of all scruple and doubtfulness: requiring

* See Cardwell's Doc. Annals, Vol. 1, p. 10.

" such, as shall be satisfied with a general Confes-
" sion, not to be offended with them that do use, to
" their further satisfying, the auricular and secret
" confession to the Priest; nor those also, which
" think needful or convenient, for the quietness of
" their own consciences, particularly to open their
" sins to the Priest, to be offended with them which
" are satisfied with their humble confession to God,
" and the general confession to the Church; but in
" all these things to follow and keep the rule of
" Charity; and every man to be satisfied with his
" own conscience, not judging other men's minds or
" acts, whereas he hath no warrant of God's word
" for the same."*

Here then is "auricular Confession," both name
and thing, expressly authorized in the very time of
the Reformation; and in the year following (A.D.
1549) we have the Book of Common Prayer, which
is commonly called the first Book of Edward VI.,
published and authorized by Act of Parliament;
and it is remarkable, that the Act of Parliament
which required the use of this Prayer Book, (Stat.
2 & 3 Edw. 6, c. 1,) declared it to have been
compiled " by the aid of the Holy Ghost." Now
in the Exhortation prefixed to the Communion
Office,† the same reference to, and sanction of, " the

* See the Two Books of Common Prayer of Edward VI.,
edited by Cardwell, p. 428.

† Ib. p. 278.

auricular and discreet confession to the Priest," is repeated in almost all the very same words, and in the Office for the Visitation of the Sick, in the same book,* there is this Rubric: " Here shall the sick " person make a special confession, if he feel his " conscience troubled with any weighty matter. " After which confession, the Priest shall absolve " him after this form; and the same form of abso- " lution shall be used in all private confessions;"— thus recognizing auricular and secret confession, not only in the case of sickness, but on other occasions.

In the 2nd Prayer Book of Edward VI., published in the year 1552, and in the later Prayer Books, revised and sanctioned in the years 1559, and 1662, these passages were in part omitted, but the Exhortation in the Communion Office, and the Rubric in the Office for the Visitation of the Sick, are equally express in encouraging special and private confession; and the same form of absolution is prescribed. Nowhere are the Laity forbidden to make, or the Clergy to receive, private confessions, but the contrary; and the power of forgiving and retaining sins, conferred at the Ordination of Priests, is tied to no time or circumstances;—and in the Homily of Repentance, (which is one of those authorized by the 39 Articles, (Art. 35,) a general liberty of resorting to the Clergy for such purposes is plainly

* Cardwell's Two Books of Common Prayer of Edward VI., p. 363.

declared. Lastly, in the 113th of the Canons of the year 1603, which the Courts of Law have declared to be binding upon the Clergy, we find the following proviso: " Provided always, that if " any man confess his secret and hidden sins to the " Minister, for the unburdening of his conscience, " and to receive spiritual consolation and ease of " mind from him, we do not any way bind the " said Minister by this our constitution," (the Canon had just provided for making presentments of crimes to the Ordinary,) " but do straitly charge " and admonish him, that he do not at any time " reveal and make known to any person whatso- " ever any crime or offence so committed to his " trust and secrecy, (except they be such crimes as " by the laws of this realm his own life may be " called into question for concealing the same,) " under pain of irregularity."

What particular crimes are here intended in this latter exception I am unable to discover; for the mere concealment of Treason, or of Felony, was no more than the offence of misprision, the stat. 1 & 2 Ph. & Ma. c. 10, s. 8, having enacted, " that con- " cealment or keeping secret of any High Treason " be deemed and taken only misprision of Treason," and the concealment of Felony being by Common Law a misdemeanor only; in neither case there- fore, neither of them being a capital offence, could the Priest's " own life be called into question for

" concealing the same," even supposing that the concealment in consequence of a religious confession would have been in any case, or at any period, a misprision in point of Law, which I venture very strongly to doubt. This exception therefore in the Canon seems in reality to amount to nothing;—while it is evident, that the Proviso was designed to give protection to religious confession generally, and to prevent any Clergyman from violating it, whether in Court or elsewhere. I must observe, however, that this Canon, although binding upon the Clergy, is not binding upon the Laity ;* and that as the secrecy of confession is the privilege, not of the Priest, but of the Penitent, the Laity may truly say, " We " know nothing about the Canon of 1603, but we " know that our confessions are privileged by the " Common Law, and by earlier Canons confirmed " by Parliament; and although this Canon of " 1603 merely requires you, the Clergy, to preserve " the secrecy of our confessions ' under pain of " irregularity,' we claim the protection of a more " stringent rule, and declare that you are bound to " keep our confessions inviolate, under the old " penalties, as confirmed long before your Canon of " 1603 was in existence."

Upon the whole, it is beyond all question, that neither the proceedings of the 16th, nor those of the 17th century, (including therefore the whole

* See Middleton v. Croft, Cases temp. Lord Hardwicke, 326.

period of the Reformation) made any change whatever in the sacred and inviolable character of this
religious Rite. They certainly did not render
unlawful the general use of private penitential
confession, and it is perfectly clear, that, both by
Parliament and by Convocation, the continuance
of it in certain cases was directly encouraged and
enjoined. It is also worthy of remark, that the
Rubric of the Book of Common Prayer, in the
Order for the Visitation of the Sick, as finally altered
and settled in the year 1662, carries this matter
further than the Rubrics in force before;—for the
former Rubric merely said, " Here shall the sick
" person make *a special confession,* if he feel his
" conscience troubled *with any weighty matter;*"—
whereas the present Rubric says, " Here shall the
" sick person be moved to make *a special confession*
" *of his sins,* if he feel his conscience troubled with
" any weighty matter,"—thereby seeming to show,
that the confession is now to be, not merely *a special
confession, confined to some particular weighty matter;*
but a special confession *of all his sins,* if he desires
to confess and receive absolution for any. And as
the Rubrics, as well as the rest, of the Book of
Common Prayer, are now part of the Law of the
Land, having been confirmed by the Stat. 13 & 14
Car. II. c. 4, the Clergy of the Established Church
are positively required, not merely to receive the con-

fessions of Penitents in certain cases, when volun-
tarily tendered, but actually to urge and exhort the
making of them, where parties may be reluctant to
make them. But if the practice has thus remained,
and been thus recognised and authorized, it will
certainly need better arguments than any which I
have ever seen advanced, to show that the privilege
of secrecy, which had before attached to it, was lost
at the Reformation. If it be said, that it was no
longer imperatively required of the members of the
Church, the answer is obvious, and, I think, conclusive, that to allow it in any case, and still more
to encourage and enjoin it in some, was equivalent
to a pledge on the part of the Church and of Parliament, that it should be attended by all the
privileges recessary to its free exercise ;— that those
privileges existed by the Law of the State, as well
as by the Law of the Church, and that there is
nothing in the Statute Book, directly or indirectly,
to annul or weaken them. If again, it be objected,
that the Sacramental character of Confession was
done away, and that therefore its inviolability was
affected, it may be replied, first, that the Sacramental character of Penance has not been denied
by the English Church, but only a lower place
assigned to it than to Baptism and the Eucharist,
the same having been the case with regard to Confirmation, Matrimony, and Orders ; 2ndly, that

granting that its sacramental character has been disparaged, it has not fared better than these other ordinances, and yet every one knows that the rules of the Canon and Common Law do generally apply to these, and if so, Why should they not apply also to Confession? 3rdly, that the absolute denial of its sacramental character would not at all destroy its privilege of secrecy, inasmuch as that privilege rests, not merely, nor even mainly, upon its sacramental character, but upon other grounds of the highest importance, the avoidance of scandal, and the necessity of secrecy to the maintenance of the Rite.

The arguments therefore which deny this privilege are utterly worthless. I do not choose to discuss here the question of its policy, although I may possibly have something to say upon that subject hereafter: I am now dealing strictly with the legal question, and on that I maintain, that the law protects it, as it has always done.

This reasoning, respecting the changes which occurred at and after the Reformation, applies of course almost entirely to the Protestant Church, then by law established on the ruins of the Catholic. The right of Catholics, at the present day, to have their confessions protected in Courts of Justice, rests upon a somewhat different ground from that of Anglicans, but not very difficult to support. That they had that right originally, by the Common Law as well as by the Laws Ecclesiastical, up to the period of the Reformation, cannot, 1 presume, be doubted. If they lost it at that time, they lost it, not because the privilege itself was taken away, or treated as illegal, by any special enactment, but because the Religion itself, of which it formed part, was proscribed, and the Priests and Professors of that Religion exposed to the most cruel persecution, under a code of Laws as tyrannical and barbarous as ever disgraced a civilized nation. The proscription of the Religion itself was the proscription of all those of its ordinances and its privileges, which were not specially retained by the new system established. But happily those days of tyranny and barbarism are ended, and the Religion is restored, not indeed as the Religion of the State, but as one sanctioned and protected by Law. The Catholic therefore is reinstated in his right to the perfect enjoyment of all the ordinances of his Creed, and of those privileges which are necessary to the performance of every one of his religious duties. If he is not, he has not that benefit which the Legislature intended to give him; for what a mockery would it be to tell him, " True it is, you are now permitted to go, " as your ancestors went, to confession, where your " religion requires you to make a full acknowledg- " ment of all your sins, and the Priest is bound to " hear you ; but remember, that he is now liable to " be called upon at any time, upon pain of impri-

" sonment, to reveal whatever you confess, and
" therefore, if unfortunately you have committed
" any heinous crime, which presses heavily upon
" your conscience, and for which you more parti-
" cularly need the consolation and advice of your
" spiritual Director, he may be made the means of
" bringing you, however deeply you may repent
" your sins, to penal servitude, or to an ignominious
" death, unless he refuses to betray his trust, and
" by his refusal to commit a breach of the Law."
But who does not see, that this would practically
be a denial altogether of the Sacrament of Penance
to the Catholic who most requires it; and if so,
that his religion is restored to him, not as his ancestors had it, but in a mutilated state and an
utterly insufficient manner?

Look again at the condition of the Priest—he is
bound, under the most solemn obligations of his
religion, never, under any circumstances, or whatever may be the demand made upon him, to reveal
any sin which a penitent has confessed to him, and
it may be perfectly true, and indeed everybody
who knows what Catholic Priests are, can testify,
that not one of them would so violate his religion
and his honour, as to be guilty of such a crime, for
all that the world could give or take away:

> " Phalaris licet imperet, ut sit
> " Falsus, et admoto dictet perjuria tauro."

But is any Priest to be exposed to the alternative, of either violating his most solemn obligations, and destroying his position and his character, or exposing himself to punishment and to prison, for refusing to violate his conscience, and his duty to God and man ? How can *he* be said to be restored to the free exercise of his religion, or to the due performance of those very duties which the Law has actually authorized him to perform ? Until I am shown some Act of Parliament, which has expressly destroyed the secrecy of religious confession, I must take the liberty of doubting, whether any Catholic can be deprived of it, as he actually had it by Law till his religion itself was exterminated, and since the free enjoyment of his religion has been restored to him, without any legislative restriction.

With respect to Protestant Dissenters, the question may possibly not be quite so easy of solution, as that respecting the members of the Established Church, or the Roman Catholics. But if there are any of them, as I believe there are some, who recognize the duty, and conform to the practice, of private religious confession, they may fairly ask, why they should not have it, with all the privileges which always belonged to it, and which are essential to its due observance ? If their forms of religion are legalised, they are entitled to protection in

the exercise of them all. The right of confession
they probably retain, as a remnant of the religious
system from which they separated at or after the
Reformation, and thus it may be deemed to have
passed to them unimpaired and unaffected, and
therefore privileged ; while the Anglican Church
itself shows, that the Reformation has not abrogated it, and that it is not inconsistent with the
religion of Protestants. In connexion with this
branch of the subject, I may quote the observations
of Mr. Best, in his able and excellent work on the
Principles of the Law of Evidence (page 694); he
says, " If the refusing to hold spiritual communica-
" tions sacred is an error, an opposite and greater
" one is the attempt to confine the privilege to the
" Clergy of some particular creed. Courts of
" Municipal Law are not called on to determine
" the truth or merits of the religious persuasion to
" which a party belongs, or to enquire whether it
" exacts auricular confession, advises, encourages,
" or permits it; the sole question for them ought
" to be, whether the party who *bonâ fide* seeks for
" spiritual advice should be allowed it *freely*. By a
" statute of New York, 'No Minister of the Gospel,
" ' or Priest, of any denomination whatsoever, shall
" ' be allowed to disclose any confessions made to him
" ' in his professional character, in the course of dis-

"' cipline enjoined by the rules or practice of such
"' denomination.' A similar statute exists in Mis-
" souri, and the like principle is recognized in
" France;" and he adds, in a note, a passage from
Bonnier's Traité des Preuves, s. 179, " Le système
" contraire détruirait la confiance, qui seule peut
" amener le repentir, en donnant au prêtre les
" apparences d'un délateur, d'autant plus odieux
" qu'il serait revêtu d'un charactère sacré."

These observations of Mr. Best relate perhaps
rather to the policy, than to the Law of this question;
but I quote them as in part confirmatory of what I
have stated, with regard to Catholics and Protestant
Dissenters,—that when the Law secures to them the
free exercise of their religion, it guarantees them
the full enjoyment of every privilege necessary to
the due observance of all its Rites; that if it intended
to make any exception or restriction, it was bound
to state it plainly, as the grant would otherwise be
a snare and a delusion;—and that the Law may now
be deemed to recognise penitential confession simply
as a religious Rite, independently of the particular
profession of Faith of which it forms part.

But it is now time to turn to the English writers
on the Law of Evidence, who have referred to this
question, and to examine their statements, and the
cases on which they rely. Amongst these, the first

in order of time appears to be Mr. Serjeant Peake, who, in his " Compendium of the Law of Evidence," says; " This rule of Professional confidence extends " only to the case of facts stated to a legal Practi- " tioner, for the purpose of enabling him to conduct " a cause ; and therefore a confession to a Clergy- " man, or a Priest, for the purpose of easing the " culprit's conscience, the statement of a man to " his private friend, or of a patient to his physician, " is not within the protection of the Law." The only authorities which he cites in support of these positions are the case of The King v. Sparkes, in Peake's Nisi Prius Cases, page 78, and the case of the Duchess of Kingston, in the 20th Volume of the State Trials.

Mr. Serjeant Peake is followed by Mr. Starkie, who, in his " Treatise on the Law of Evidence," after mentioning the privilege which exempts counsel, solicitors, and attorneys, from divulging " any matter which has been communicated to " them in professional confidence," says,† " All other " Professional Persons, whether Physicians, Sur- " geons, or Divines, are bound to disclose the secrets " which have been reposed in them in the practice " of their professions, when called upon to do so for " the purposes of justice. It has been held, that a

---

* Peake on Evid. p. 180.
† Stark. on Evid. vol. ii. p. 322.

" Roman Catholic Priest is bound to reveal secrets
" confided to him in the course of confession."

In support of these propositions, Mr. Starkie cites
the cases of Wilson v. Rastall, 4 T. R. 753; Rex v.
Duchess of Kingston, 11 State Tr. 243; and those
reported in 1 Keb. Rep. 505, 1 Vent. 197, Skinner,
404; Peake's Cases, 77; Butler v. Moore, before
Sir Mich. Smith, Master of the Rolls, Macnally,
253; Vaillant v. Dodemead, 2 Atk. 524; and Bac.
Ab. Evidence, A. 2.

Mr. Phillips, in his Treatise, after saying, that
" The professional privilege is confined to the cases
" which have been enumerated," (those of Barristers, Attorneys, and Solicitors,)* adds, " a con-
" fession to a Clergyman is not privileged," for
which he refers to the case of " The King v. Sparkes,
" cited in Du Barré v. Livette, Peake, 77," observing, " the confession was made by a Papist." He
then adds, in a note, " In Broad v. Pitt, 3 C. & P.
" 519, Lord Wynford said that it had been decided
" in Gilham's Case, R. & M. Cr. Cas. 194, that the
" privilege did not extend to Clergymen, but that
" he would never compel a Clergyman to disclose
" communications made to him by a prisoner, but
" if he chose to disclose them, he should receive
" them in evidence. He also observed, that the
" confidence in the case of Attorneys was a great

* Phill. on Evid. vol. i. pp. 176, 177.

" anomaly in the Law. A confession to a Popish
" Priest has been held not to be privileged—Butler
" v. Moore, Macnally, 253. In Du Barré v.
" Livette, Peake, 108, Lord Kenyon apparently
" dissents from the decision in R. v. Sparkes."

Mr. Roscoe, in his " Digest of the Law of Evidence in Criminal Cases,"* after speaking of the
privilege of Counsel, &c., says, " Other professional
" persons, whether Physicians, Surgeons, or Clergy-
" men, have no such privilege," for which he refers
to the cases of Wilson v. Rastall, and the Duchess
of Kingston's Case, already cited by the writers
just noticed. He then goes on,—" Thus, where
" the prisoner, being a Roman Catholic, made a
" confession, before a Protestant Clergyman, of the
" crime for which he was indicted, that confession
" was permitted to be given in evidence at the trial,
" and he was convicted and executed.—Sparkes'
" Case, cited Peake, N. P. C. 78. Upon this case
" being cited, Lord Kenyon observed, that he
" should have paused before he admitted the evi-
" dence ; but there appears to be no ground for
" this doubt. In Gilham's Case, Ry. & M. C. C. R.
" 198, it was admitted by the counsel for the pri-
" soner, that a Clergyman is bound to disclose
" what has been revealed to him as matter of

* Roscoe on Criminal Evid. p. 175.

" religious confession, and the prisoner in that case
" was convicted and executed."

Mr. Pitt Taylor, in his masterly work on
Evidence,* lays down the law thus :—" Clergymen and Medical Men are bound to disclose any
" information, which, by acting in their professional
" character, they have confidentially acquired."
And he afterwards says : " Though the Law of
" England encourages the Penitent to confess his
" sins, for the unburthening of his conscience,
" and to receive spiritual consolation and ease of
" mind, yet the Minister, to whom the confession
" is made, is merely excused from presenting the
" offender to the Civil Magistrate, and enjoined
" not to reveal the matter confessed, under pain of
" irregularity. In all other respects, he is left to
" the full operation of the rules of the Common
" Law, which recognize no distinction between
" Clergymen and Laymen, but provide that all
" confessions and other matters, not confided to
" legal counsel, must be disclosed, when required
" for the purposes of justice. Neither penitential
" confessions made to the Minister, or to members
" of the party's own Church, nor even secrets con-
" fided to a Roman Catholic Priest in the course of
" confession, are regarded as privileged communi-
" cations." And he cites in proof of his statements,

* Taylor on Evid. vol. ii. pp. 755, 756, 757, 3rd ed.

" Rex *v.* Gilham, 1 Moo. C. C. 186; Butler *v.*
" Moore, Macnally's Ev. 253 – 255; Anon., Skin.
" 404; Du Barré *v.* Livette, Peak. R. 77; Com *v.*
" Drake, 15 Mass. 161 :" and in a note he refers to
the dictum of Lord Chief Justice Best, in Broad *v.*
Pitt, 3 C. & P. 519, and M. & M. 234, S. C.,
which I have already given. He also adds, "in
" R. *v.* Griffin, 6 Cox, Cr. Cas. 219, Baron Alder-
" son is reported to have gone further, and to have
" expressed an opinion, that communications made
" by a prisoner to a Clergyman ought not to be
" disclosed."

Mr. Best, in his "Treatise on the Principles of Evidence,"* to which I have already referred, states the
Law on this subject with far greater caution, and, as
will be seen, with far greater accuracy. His words
are these : " Whether communications made to Cler-
" gymen by persons applying for spiritual advice are,
" or should be, protected from disclosure in Courts
" of Justice, presents a question of some difficulty.
" It is commonly. thought that the decisions of the
" Judges in the cases of Rex *v.* Gilham and Rex *v.*
" Wild, added to some others that will be cited per-
" sently, have determined it in the negative, and
" the practice is in accordance with that notion.
" But the former of these cases only shows, that a
" confession of guilt, made by a prisoner to the

* Best on Evid. p. 690.

" world, or a Magistrate, in consequence of the
" spiritual exhortations of a Clergyman that it will
" be for his soul's health to do so, is receivable in
" evidence against him—a decision perfectly well
" founded, because such exhortations cannot pos-
" sibly be considered illegal ' inducements to con-
" ' fess.' By this expression, as shown in a former
" chapter, the law means language calculated to
" convey to the mind of a person suspected of an
" offence, that, by confessing, he will better his
" position with reference to the *temporal* conse-
" quences of that offence. And the ground on
" which a Confession made after such an induce-
" ment to confess is rejected is, the reasonable
" apprehension that, in consequence, the party
" may have made a false acknowledgment of guilt,
" an argument wholly inapplicable where he is
" only told that a *spiritual* benefit is to be derived
" from telling the truth. The case of Rex *v.* Wild
" is even less to the purpose; as the party who
" used the exhortation there neither was, nor pro-
" fessed to be, a Clergyman, and, wholly un-
" solicited, thrust it on the prisoner. The other
" cases to which allusion has been made are an
" anonymous one in Skinner, Rex *v.* Sparkes,
" Butler *v.* Moore, and Wilson *v.* Rastall. In the
" first the question was respecting a confidential
" communication to a Man of Law, which Lord

" Chief Justice Holt, as might have been expected,
" held privileged from disclosure, adding *obiter* that
" ' it was otherwise in the case of a Gentleman,
" ' Parson, &c." The second and third are decisions,
" one by Buller, J., on circuit, and the other by the
" Irish Master of the Rolls in 1802, that confessions
" to a Protestant and a Roman Catholic Clergyman
" respectively are not privileged; and in the fourth
" the Judges in banc say *obiter*, that the privilege
" is confined to the cases of Counsel, Solicitor, and
" Attorney. How far a particular form of religious
" belief, being disfavoured by Law at the period,
" affected the latter of those decisions, is not easy
" to say; but both of them leave the general ques-
" tion untouched; and on Rex *v.* Sparkes being
" cited to Lord Kenyon in Du Barré *v.* Livette,
" he said, ' I should have paused before I admitted
" the evidence then admitted.' He however
" decided that case on the ground, that confidential
" communications to a legal adviser were distin-
" guishable from others. It is also to be observed,
" that the subject coming incidentally before Best,
" C. J., in Broad *v.* Pitt, very shortly after Rex *v.*
" Gilham, he referred to that case, as deciding that
" the privilege in question did not apply to a
" Clergyman; but added, ' I, for one, will never
" ' compel a Clergyman to disclose communications

" ' made to him by a prisoner; but if he chooses to
" ' disclose them, I shall receive them in evidence.' "

Mr. Best then adds, " There cannot, we appre-
" hend be much doubt, that, previous to the Refor-
" mation, statements made to a Priest under the
" Seal of Confession were privileged from dis-
" closure, except perhaps when the matter thus
" communicated amounted to High Treason. In
" the old laws of Henry I. is this passage, ' Caveat
" ' sacerdos ne de hiis qui ei confitentur peccata
" ' sua alicui recitet quod ei confessus est, non
" ' propinquis, non extraneis; quod si fecerit,
" ' deponatur, et omnibus diebus vitæ suæ ignomi-
" ' niosus peregrinando pœniteat.' The laws of
" Henry I. are of course not binding per se, and
" are only valuable as guides to the Common Law,
" but it is otherwise with the Statute Articuli Cleri
" (9 Edw. 2, c. 10), which is as follows." He then
sets out the passage of this Statute which I have
already quoted, and afterwards the Commentary of
Lord Coke, which I have also given at length; and
concludes by saying, " This passage has been cited
" to prove the Common Law on this subject, but
" we much doubt whether the caveat at the end of
" the above enactment, (' caveant confessores ne
" ' erronice hujusmodi appellatores informent,') was
" inserted to warn the Confessor against disclosing

" the secrets of the Penitent *to others.* The gram-
" matical construction and context seem to show,
" that it was to prevent his abusing his privilege of
" access to the criminal by conveying information
" to him from without, and the clause is translated
" accordingly in the best editions of the Statutes."

Such are the statements made by these various
writers upon this important subject, amongst whom
Mr. Best evidently differs, very widely, from all the
others. I shall now examine in their order the
several authorities which are relied upon by those,
who deny the right of the Clergy to withhold the
evidence of what they have heard in Confession.
These authorities are, as we have seen,—Sparke *v.*
Sir Hugh Middleton, 1 Keb. Rep. 505; Cuts *v.*
Pickering, and Jones *v.* The Countess of Man-
chester, 1 Vent. Rep. 197; An Anonymous Case,
Skinn. Rep. 404; Bac. Abr. tit. Evidence, A. 2;
Vaillant *v.* Dodemead, 2 Atkins' Rep. 524; The
Duchess of Kingston's Case, 20 How. State Trials,
573; The King *v.* Sparkes, cited in Peake's N. P.
Cas. 78; Wilson *v.* Rastall, 4 T. R. 753; Rex *v.*
Gilham, Moo. C. C. R. 186; Rex *v.* Wild, Moo.
C.C. R. 452; Butler *v.* Moore, Macnally on Ev. 253.

Now the three first of these cases are cited by
Mr. Starkie alone, as supporting his statement on
this subject; and I certainly am at a loss to see how
they bear upon it at all. The case of Sparke *v.* Sir

E

Hugh Middleton relates merely to the disclosures
which counsel are exempted from making, and says
nothing, even incidentally, about any other persons
whatever. That of Cuts *v.* Pickering has not the
most remote reference to any person, except a solicitor; and that of Jones *v.* The Countess of Man-
chester relates only to the liability of a trustee to
produce certain documents, Lord Chief Justice Hale
observing *obiter*, " that it was against the duty of a
" counsellor or solicitor, &c., to discover the evi-
" dence which he who retains him acquaints him
" with." These cases therefore are not in point
in the slightest degree, for nothing is said in any
one of them respecting any minister of religion, nor
does any one lay down any general rule, or allude
to the evidence of any other person than those enumerated.

The anonymous case in Skinner's Reports is not
of much value, though cited both by Mr. Starkie
and by Mr. Pitt Taylor, and it really lays down no
generally exclusive rule. It was a mere Nisi Prius
case, in which the only question was, whether an
attorney should be compelled to disclose the nature
of a corrupt agreement, which he had been employed to prepare, and Lord Holt held that he
should not; the report then adds; "it seems to
" be the same law of a scrivener, and he (Lord
" Holt) cited a case, where, upon a covenant to
" convey as counsel should advise, and ' counsel

" ' did not advise' being pleaded, conveyances made
" by the advice of a scrivener were allowed to be
" good evidence upon this issue, for he is a counsel
" to a man with whom he will advise, if he be
" instructed and educated in such way of practice ;
" otherwise of a Gentleman, Parson, &c." Now
independently of this being a mere *obiter dictum*
of a Judge at Nisi Prius, it is evident that Lord
Holt was not considering, or referring to, the case
of a Clergyman entrusted by a Penitent in matters
of spiritual concern—his words really are only applicable to the subject before him, and simply mean,
that if a Gentleman, a Parson, or any other person,
not educated or practising as a Lawyer, is consulted
on matters which properly belong only to a man
professionally educated as a Lawyer, the communications made between such persons cannot be
considered professional—in other words, the Gentleman, or the Parson, cannot be treated as a Lawyer,
though he has apparently acted in that capacity.

This case therefore has no more bearing than the
other three upon the question now under consideration, and it is only extraordinary, that they should
have been adduced at all, as connected with the
subject of Religious Confessions.

The passage in Bacon's Abridgment, to which
only Mr. Starkie has referred, amounts to nothing;
for the original text of Bacon states merely the

privilege of "Counsellors, Attorneys, and Soli-
" citors," without any exclusion of other persons.   The Editor Gwillim indeed has added
to Bacon's text, and says, " This privilege is con-
" fined to the cases of Counsel, Solicitor and
" Attorney, and does not extend to any other
" Piofessions ;" but he has given no authority
for this, except the Duchess of Kingston's Case
in the State Trials, and the case of Wilson
v. Rastall in Term Reports, each of which I shall
consider presently, and show that it is irrelevant.

The case of Vaillant v. Dodemead is next in
order.   It was a case in Chancery before Lord
Hardwicke, respecting a collusive assignment of a
lease, and a question arising upon a demurrer to
certain interrogatories, which had been administered
to a Mr. Bristow, " Clerk in Court in the Cause,"
the Lord Chancellor, in considering the objections
made to the demurrer, said, " The third objection
" is, that it is too general ; for the words are, that
" he knew nothing but as Clerk in Court, or Agent.
" Now, the word *agent* is very extensive and un-
" certain, for no persons are privileged from being
" examined in such cases, but persons of the Pro-
" fession, as Counsel, Solicitor, or Attorney, for an
" Agent may be only a Steward, or Servant."
Now Lord Hardwicke cannot fairly be supposed to

have meant more than he actually said, and by using the words, " in such cases," he showed that his attention was confined to cases of the same nature as the one before him : he did not refer to cases of a totally different kind, still less to cases foreign to his own jurisdiction. Had he done so, his observations would have been entirely extra-judicial, and consequently of no importance. Lord Hardwicke was simply determining the meaning of the word " *agent*," and showing that it was too *generic*, and might include unprivileged persons. It is as if he had said, " By the word ' agent,' I " cannot understand a *legal* agent, as it may mean " a steward, or a servant, neither of whom has any " privilege ; I cannot hold it to mean a Barrister, " Solicitor, or Attorney, who properly constitute " ' the Profession,' and who therefore are alone " entitled, in cases like the present, to the pri-" vilege of a professional or legal agent." And this construction makes his language analogous to that of Lord Holt, in the case in Skinner's Reports just mentioned, that a person consulted, and assuming to advise, as a Lawyer, cannot claim the privilege of a Lawyer, if he is not really a member of the Profession. Lord Hardwicke certainly cannot be deemed to have laid down any general rule, or to have even expressed an opinion upon matters which were not before him, or to have interfered with principles not submitted to his notice;—particularly when it is remembered, that no authority before Lord Hardwicke's time can be adduced to show, that the privilege in question was *confined* to the legal profession;—certainly not one that affected in any way the rights of Ministers of Religion, with respect to Confessions made to them;—the previous cases, so far as I can discover, having only decided that Barristers, Solicitors, and Attorneys *are* privileged, not that other classes generally *are not*.

The case of Vaillant v. Dodemead therefore does not touch the present question.

The Duchess of Kingston's case, in the State Trials, has been used to support the view of those, who confine this privilege to members of the Legal Profession. But it does nothing of the kind;—it lays down no general rule;—and so far from deciding that Priests and Ministers of Religion have no privilege, it says nothing whatever about them. The only persons, whose privilege was considered at all in that case, were a Surgeon, a Peer, and an Attorney. The question relating to the Surgeon occurred first, upon the objection of Mr. Cæsar Hawkins to disclose certain matters, which had come to his knowledge professionally: the objection was not argued, nor was there any discussion about it; but, Lord Mansfield intimating the opinion of the House of Lords, " that a Surgeon has no privi-" lege to avoid giving evidence in a Court of Jus-

" tice, but is bound by the Law of the land to do
" it," Mr. Hawkins gave his evidence without further hesitation. The next question was as to the
liability of a Peer to give evidence, who had been a
friend of the prisoner, and claimed to be relieved
from disclosing what he thought that his honour
required him to conceal. The House decided that
he was bound to answer, the prisoner herself at the
same time releasing him from all obligation to
silence. The last question related merely to the
extent of an Attorney's privilege, the witness
leaving it to the House to say, whether the matter
on which he was examined was matter which,
as an Attorney, he was bound to testify. There is
not therefore, in the whole of the Duchess of Kingston's case, what the writers on evidence have
assumed that it contains : it is confined entirely to
the points which I have mentioned, and consequently is no authority for anything beyond them.

The case of Wilson v. Rastall, which related
only to an Attorney, has been also cited, for the
same purpose as the Duchess of Kingston's Case ;
—and the language of Mr. Justice Buller has been
much relied upon. That learned Judge there says,
" This doctrine of privilege was fully discussed in
" a case before Lord Hardwicke. The privilege
" is confined to Counsel, Solicitor, and Attorney ;
" but, in order to raise the privilege, it must be

" proved, that the information, which the adverse
" party wishes to learn, was communicated to the
" witness in one of those characters; for if he be
" employed merely as a steward, he may be ex-
" amined." And subsequently he observes, " I
" take the distinction to be now well settled, that
" the privilege extends to those three enumerated
" cases at all times, but that it is confined to those
" cases only. There are cases to which it is much
" to be lamented that the law of privilege is
" not extended; those in which medical persons
" are obliged to disclose the information which
" they acquire, by attending in their professional
" characters. This point was very much considered
" in the Duchess of Kingston's Case, when Sir
" C. Hawkins, who had attended the Duchess as a
" medical person, made the objection himself, but
" was overruled, and compelled to give evidence
" against the prisoner."

It is evident, that in making these observations,
the learned Judge went much further than he was
justified in doing :—In the first place, when he said,
that " this doctrine of privilege was fully discussed
before Lord Hardwicke," he very much overstated
the fact;—for if he referred, as it is clear that he
did, to the case of Vaillant v. Dodemead, there is
nothing in the report of that case which shows,
that the doctrine was really *discussed* at all,—for,

the report, as I have already shown, contains only
the Demurrer, with the formal objections to it,
and the Lord Chancellor's judgment thereon : and
as to the observation, that " the privilege was
confined to the three enumerated cases only,"— I
would ask, when and where had it ever been so
confined ? No reported decision, before Lord
Hardwicke's, had so confined it, and that decision,
as we have seen, does not warrant any such construction. Even if it did, it would not by any
means have " settled " the law, for it must be
remembered, that Lord Hardwicke's decision, as
well as this of Mr. Justice Buller, was, so far as it
may be supposed to have laid down any general
and exclusive rule, entirely extrajudicial,—for the
case before each of the Judges related solely to the
privilege of a legal agent, or attorney, not to that
of any other persons. Again, when Mr. Justice
Buller said, that the privilege of medical persons
had been " very much considered in the Duchess of
Kingston's Case," he stated what was not true ;—
for the report in the State Trials shows, that, upon
Mr. Hawkins objecting to give evidence, the Lord
High Steward put the question to the Lords, without having it " considered," or argued, at all, and
that Mr. Hawkins yielded his objection at once,
when Lord Mansfield suggested that the Lords
considered him bound to answer.

Mr. Justice Buller's authority therefore, in Wilson
v. Rastall, for the doctrine for which it is cited,
loses all its importance, when it is shown, not only
that his observations were extrajudicial, but that
the cases to which he referred fail to support his
statements.

The next case is that of The King v. Sparkes, a
case which the more I consider, the more astonished
I am that any stress has ever been laid upon it:—
we have no report of the case,—we are not even
told when or where it occurred, except that it was
somewhere upon the Northern Circuit;—we know
nothing of the circumstances under which the confession referred to was made; or of the reasons on
which it was received in evidence;—*all the knowledge of it which we have is derived from a casual
reference to it, in an argument of the plantiff's
counsel, in a Nisi Prius case,* before Lord Kenyon,—
when Mr. Garrow, (who was not a member of the
Northern Circuit, and therefore most probably
knew nothing about it, except from some very imperfect statement,) in arguing for the admissibility
of a witness, who had acted as an interpreter
between the defendant (a foreigner) and his attorney, said, that " a case much stronger than that
" had been determined by Mr. Justice Buller, on
" the Northern Circuit. It was a case in which
" the life of the prisoner was at stake. The

" name of it was The King v. Sparkes. There
" the prisoner, being a Papist, had made a confes-
" sion, before a Protestant Clergyman, of the crime
" for which he was indicted, and that confession
" was permitted to be given in evidence on the trial,
" and he was convicted and executed. The reason
" against admitting that evidence (continued the
" learned Counsel) was much stronger than in
" the case then before the Court ; there the prisoner
" came to the Priest for ghostly comfort, and to ease
" his conscience, oppressed with guilt." Now, independently of the extreme looseness and insuffi-
ciency of this statement, and of our entire ignorance
of some of the most important facts,—an ignorance
which renders it impossible to be relied upon,—there
is one very obvious remark to be made, which at
once almost disposes of it. The confession was
made by a Catholic prisoner to a Protestant Clergyman,—and such a confession, as every Catholic
knows, would not be a Sacramental Confession, or
made, under the Seal of Confession, to a person
whom the penitent would deem competent to give
him absolution. The presumption therefore is, that
this confession, though possibly made, as the Counsel suggested, " for ghostly comfort, and to ease his
" conscience oppressed with guilt," was not one
which the prisoner expected, or even wished, to be
concealed,—and the Protestant Clergyman, in di-

vulging it, most probably had reason to believe, (and it must be hoped, for his own sake, that he had,) that he was not violating any secret confidence, or acting a base or dishonourable part. Such a state of things is not uncommon; and we shall presently see, in the case of the King v. Gilham, that a confession was made in a manner somewhat similar, and was very properly received in evidence. This consideration alone is sufficient to show, that the case of the King v. Sparkes is no authority for the position which it is commonly cited to support; independently of the fact, that there are no circumstances stated on which any reliance can be placed; and that the little value which it might have been supposed to have possessed is neutralized by the declared opinion of Lord Kenyon, who, when it was cited, expressed his dissatisfaction with Mr. Justice Buller's decision;—Mr. Justice Buller being a Judge, whose views upon this subject of privilege, as we have already seen, were by no means accurate or trustworthy. At all events, the case shows nothing as to the obligation of a Priest or Minister to disclose any religious confession, or any confidential communication; for the Protestant Clergyman may have volunteered his testimony, being under no moral obligation to withhold it, and not having had it extorted from him by any compulsion or order of the Court.

The case of the King *v.* Gilham, to which I just
now adverted, has been frequently, and, I may say,
unaccountably supposed to prove, that "Clergymen are bound to disclose any information, which,
by acting in their professional character, they have
confidentially acquired." But any person who
takes the trouble of reading it must see at once,
that it proves no such thing; and it is astonishing
that the case should have been so much misunder-
stood as it has been. The prisoner Gilham was
charged with murder, and, soon after his commit-
ment, the gaoler, in one or two interviews with
him, and the Chaplain of the gaol, in several,
worked very strongly upon his conscience, and
urged upon him the duty of repentance, and the
confession of his guilt. These conversations the
Chaplain, who seems to have had very little knowledge of his duty, reported at once to the Magistrates;—and the prisoner, agitated by all that had
been said to him, at length confessed the crime, not
however to the Chaplain in the first instance, but
to the gaoler, and then to the Mayor and the Town
Clerk. These confessions were received in evidence
at the trial, and the only question respecting them
on that occasion, and upon an argument afterwards
before the Judges upon a case reserved, was,
whether they were legally admissible, in consequence of their having been almost extorted from

the prisoner by the manner in which he had been
previously worked upon by the gaoler and the
Chaplain;—no question was raised as to the legal
obligation of the Chaplain to give the evidence
which he had given, or to disclose any confidential
communications of the prisoner;—in fact there was
no opportunity for any such question, as the Chaplain had, long before the trial, of his own accord,
openly stated all that had passed between himself
and the prisoner; and nothing which related either
to the duty, or to the conduct, of the Chaplain was
even once alluded to by the Judges. With this
explanation the case of the King v. Gilham may be
dismissed, as it has been completely misrepresented,
and did not in fact settle, or even raise, the point
for which it has been cited. The admissions of
counsel, to which Mr. Roscoe alludes, in the statement which I have quoted from his work, are
nothing to the purpose;—and the prisoner was
convicted and executed, not in consequence of a
religious confession, made in secret confidence to a
Priest, or Minister, and revealed by him, as Mr.
Roscoe would lead his readers to suppose, but upon
admissions of guilt, made to the gaoler and to the
Magistrates, and brought about, partly by remorse
of conscience, and partly by religious exhortations
urged a good while before. The observation
therefore, respecting the effect of the decision in

Gilham's Case, reported to have been made by Lord Wynford, and referred to by Mr. Phillips, if made at all, was evidently made under a mistake, and at all events was an entirely extrajudicial remark. I must not however dismiss the case of Rex v. Gilham, without noticing another, which was cited by the prisoner's Counsel in his argument before the Judges, the case of Rex v. Radford, tried at Exeter Summer Assizes in the year 1823, before Lord Chief Justice Best, the prisoner being indicted for murder. In that case, a Clergyman had prevailed upon the prisoner to confess, by dwelling on the heinousness of the crime with which he was charged, and the denunciations of Scripture against it, without giving him any caution that it would be used in evidence against him ; and the Lord Chief Justice refused to allow the Clergyman to state the confession, saying, " that he thought " it dangerous, after the confidence thus created, " which would throw the prisoner off his guard, " and the impression thus produced, to allow " what he then said to be given in evidence against " him."

Upon this case I will only observe, that although perhaps it does not amount to much, on either side of the present question, particularly as we do not know all the circumstances under which the confession was made, it tends at least to show, as does the case of Broad v. Pitt, the leaning of the learned

Judge's mind against the reception of such confessions in evidence, when made to Clergymen in the discharge of their professional duties ;—and, at all events, the case, so far as it goes, appears to be more in point, and more favourable to my argument, than the case of Rex *v.* Gilham is either apposite or adverse to it.

The case of the King *v.* Wild has been mentioned, but is, if possible, even more irrelevant than the case of the King *v.* Gilham ; for the question there turned upon the admissibility of certain confessions of the prisoner, a boy under fourteen years of age, which had not been made to any Minister of Religion, and respecting which no Minister of Religion gave, or was asked to give, or was capable of giving, any evidence whatever. They were confessions made to some of the prisoner's own friends and neighbours, who had gathered round him at the inn to which he had been taken soon after his apprehension, and who, in a solemn manner, had desired him to kneel down and tell the truth,—and these, or similar, statements the prisoner had repeated the next day to the innkeeper's son, before his removal to the gaol. There was nothing in them of a confidential nature, as regarded either the communications themselves, or the persons to whom they were made, and it is really absurd to cite the case as having the slightest bearing upon this subject.

These are the only English cases on which the
writers on Evidence appear to rely, for their exclusion of Priests and Ministers of Religion from the
privilege contended for. The examination of them,
I think, has shown, that they do not by any means
establish the rule which those writers lay down. In
not one of them, has the question of clerical privilege
ever been fairly raised by argument, or settled by
solemn decision. Of the only two relating expressly
to Clergymen, and supposed to be adverse to the
privilege, one, the case of The King v. Gilham,
has no bearing upon the question at all ; the other,
the case of The King v. Sparkes, is so imperfectly
reported, that no reliance can be placed upon it, and
it is quite consistent with the supposition that the
Clergyman volunteered his testimony, and was justified in giving it ;—the rest, with one exception, in
which the claims of a Surgeon and of a Peer were
in question, were cases relating to Attorneys and
legal advisers ; and although, in some of these, the
rule was stated to be, that the privilege was confined
to members of the Legal Profession, it is clear that
no mere casual expressions of Judges, however dis-
tinguished, no extrajudicial statements of law, without argument or consideration, are of any real value.
Many such statements may possibly be found in
other cases, as, for instance, in the judgments of
Baron Wood and Baron Garrow, in the case of

F

Lord Falmouth *v.* Moss, (11 Price's Rep. 455), where the question related only to the privilege of a steward; and in Lord Brougham's judgment in the case of Greenough *v.* Gaskell (1 M. & K. 103), which respected the privilege of an attorney; if indeed Lord Brougham can be considered to have made any statement upon this point, when he said merely, that " it might not be very easy to discover, " why a like privilege had been refused to others, " especially to medical advisers." But in answer to them it may be asked, why, if none but legal advisers are privileged, and such has always been the rule of the Common Law, have separate questions been raised, so often as they have been, respecting different classes of persons, as Clerks, Bankers, Medical Men, Stewards, Friends, and others, for whom the same privilege has been claimed, and the claim considered open to argument? If separate arguments and decisions were necessary in these cases, the supposed rule cannot have been generally admitted, or even generally known; and if its existence has to be thus proved by a sort of process of exhaustion, the proof, so far as it relates to Priests and Ministers of Religion, is evidently still incomplete, and it has yet to be applied to them. If, again, this exclusive rule was not promulgated before the time of Lord Hardwicke, how can it be said to have been a rule of the Common Law? or, if it was a rule, how happens it that the earliest English writers on Evidence say

nothing about it ?   Lord Chief Baron Gilbert,
whose Treatise is lauded as almost faultless by
Blackstone,* does not mention it, nor does Blackstone himself, though they both speak of barristers,
solicitors, and attorneys, as privileged.   Perhaps
those who have succeeded them have supposed, that
by this " expressio unius" they intended the " ex-
" clusio alterius;" but such an inference cannot be
admitted,—they probably meant no more than this,
that they knew that the Lawyers' privilege had been
expressly decided, but that they declined to pro-
nounce upon that of others, where they had no
such decisions to guide them.

This dearth of authority, however, in the English
Courts, and in English writers, has been supposed
to be compensated by an Irish case, which is reported in Macnally's Rules of Evidence, page 253,
and occurred before the Master of the Rolls in
Ireland, in the year 1802.   It is the case of Butler
v. Brown, in which the question being one respecting the validity of Lord Dunboyne's Will, the
Catholic Priest, who had attended him in his last
illness, was called to say, whether he had died a
Catholic. The Priest refused to give evidence of what
he declared to be " a confidential communication,
" made to him in the exercise of his clerical func-
" tions." *It was admitted that there had been no*

* 3 Bla. Com. p. 367, note.

F 2

previous decision upon the subject, and the refusal of the Priest was defended on the analogy of other cases of privilege, and on the inconsistency which would exist in the law, if it sanctioned, or even tolerated, the Roman Catholic Religion, and at the same time compelled its ministers to violate the tenets of that Religion, by betraying the confidence reposed in them. The Master of the Rolls, however, decided against the privilege of the Priest, " thinking " the analogy of the cases not so strong, and the " principle on which the privilege was claimed not " so clear, as to justify him in deciding otherwise."

This is the whole substance of this case, so far as it can be collected from the very imperfect report of it which alone exists; and I can scarcely suppose, that even in Ireland it is deemed of much value. It was admitted to be a case " of the first impres- " sion," and seems to have been very imperfectly and inadequately argued ; it was decided only by a single Judge, of no great judicial eminence ; and the judgment, as reported, is about as meagre and un- satisfactory as any judgment can well be :—It rests upon no principle ; it cites no authority ; it contains no careful balancing of arguments; it ignores alto- gether the rights which a Priest might possess by the Common Law ; it shows no attempt to elicit truth, either by legal reasoning, or by historical research : " sit pro ratione voluntas" seems to be its utmost effect. Taking it therefore in the full sense, in which it seems to have been understood by the writers on Evidence, I think it of no importance, as it certainly is not binding in any Court of Law or Equity in England, and it has no such intrinsic merit, as to give it any independent authority.

But it is most material to observe, that the case does not really meet the point for which it has been so often cited; for the reason alleged by the Priest, for his refusal to give the required evidence, is in no respect conclusive or sufficient. He is merely reported to have said, that what he was asked, " was " a confidential communication made to him in the " exercise of his clerical functions." It does not appear, that it was a matter *revealed to him in Confession;*—in fact it is most probable that it was not;— or that, although possibly it had been alluded to in Confession, it was one which he was strictly bound by the rules of the Church to conceal, for he might have known it quite independently of any Confession, or simply as a confidential friend, in either of which cases the rule does not apply.

The case therefore cannot be cited as any authority to prove, that religious Confessions are not privileged, for it falls completely short of this. With these observations I feel that I may safely discard it.

I have thus examined all the cases which have been referred to by the writers on Evidence, to establish the rule which they have laid down, with the exception of one, to which Mr. Pitt Taylor refers, an American case, Com. *v.* Drake, 15 Mass. 161, which I have not been able to find. But an American case, relating to a question like the present, which must be governed entirely by English law, cannot possibly be of the slightest importance either way, and therefore it is unnecessary to notice it. I ought, however, in justice to that learned writer, to say, that he has candidly mentioned, as opposed to his view, not only the opinion of Lord Chief Justice Best in the case of Broad *v.* Pitt, already noticed, but also that of Baron Alderson in the case of the King *v.* Griffin, which is reported in the 6th volume of Cox's Criminal Cases, p. 219. In this latter case, a woman, who was charged with the murder of her child, had had frequent conversations with the Chaplain of the Workhouse, of which she had been an inmate, who had visited her, as her spiritual adviser, to administer the consolations of religion. When he was called to give evidence of what had passed, Baron Alderson said, " I think that these conversations " ought not to be given in evidence. The principle " upon which an Attorney is prevented from di- " vulging what passes with his client is because,

" without unfettered means of communication, the
" client would not have proper legal assistance.
" The same principle applies to a person, deprived
" of whose advice the prisoner would not have
" proper spiritual assistance. I do not lay this
" down as an absolute rule, but I think that such
" evidence ought not to be given."

There is therefore no authority, in any one of
these cases, for asserting, that any Minister of Religion is bound to disclose in evidence any matter
which has been revealed to him in Confession.
The point, I repeat, has never been so decided,—it
has never been argued,—it has not even been
raised ;—and we have seen that some eminent
Judges have strongly discountenanced it. I ought
however to notice a case, which occurred at the
Lent Assizes for the County of Durham, in the year
1860, before Mr. Justice Hill, then one of the
Judges of the Court of Queen's Bench. The case,
I believe, has not been reported, except in the
newspapers of the time, and it appears to have been
this :—A prisoner was indicted for stealing a watch,
which had been restored to the prosecutor by a
policeman, who had received it from the Reverend
John Kelly, the Catholic Priest of the district in
which the robbery had been committed. Mr.
Kelly was called as a witness, and, being asked
from whom he had received the watch, stated that

he " had received it in connection with the Confes-
" sional:" the Judge then said, " You are not asked
" at present to disclose anything stated to you in the
" Confessional; you are asked a simple fact, from
" whom did you receive that watch which you gave
" to the policeman?" To which the witness answered, " The reply to that question would implicate
" the person who gave me the watch, therefore I
" cannot answer it. If I answered it, my suspension
" for life would be a necessary consequence; I
" should be violating the Laws of the Church, as
" well as the natural Laws." The Judge rejoined,
" On the ground I have stated to you, you are not
" asked to disclose anything which a penitent may
" have said to you in the Confessional, but you are
" asked to disclose from whom you received stolen
" property, on the 25th of December last? Do you
" answer it, or not?" On the witness saying, that
he really could not, the Judge at once adjudged
him guilty of contempt of Court, and ordered him
to be committed to gaol.

Now, with all due respect for Mr. Justice Hill,
who, I have no doubt, acted quite conscienti-
ously, I must take the liberty of holding, that
he had no more right to commit this witness
to prison, than he had to commit any other
person in the Court. Doubtless he was mis-
led by some of those statements of the writers

on Evidence, which I have shown to be without foundation. No objection was made at the time to his conduct, although it was commented upon in very severe terms, not only in the Provincial, but also in several of the London, newspapers, and in an excellent letter from one of the jurymen, which was published immediately afterwards : for the Priest was a person universally respected and beloved, and the treatment which he received excited very general indignation. The Judge, however, (and this is very material,) did not venture to insist upon the disclosure of what the witness had been *told* in the Confessional, but drew an utterly absurd and untenable distinction, between what was *said* and what was *done* in Confession, or as the witness stated, " in connection with the Confessional;"—a distinction, which, as the juryman very sensibly remarked in his letter, "was defective in casuistry;" —for it is evident, that what is done in Confession, or an act to which the Penitent makes the Priest a party, in the immediate fulfilment of the satisfaction enjoined, and as part of the Penance prescribed, and which the Priest cannot disclose, without betraying what has been confessed to him, or compromising in some degree the position or character of the Penitent, must be as much under the Seal of Confession as anything which has been said. But the Judge did make the distinction ; and therefore the case, so far as it is worth anything, rather favours than opposes the position which I maintain.

The supposed adverse authorities being thus removed, the rule, so confidently and inconsiderately based upon them, falls of course with them, and the right which originally existed by the Common Law remains clear, unimpeached, and unimpeachable. We have seen that, from the earliest ages of the Christian Church, the Seal of Confession was annexed inviolably, and under the most solemn sanctions, to the Rite of Confession itself;—that it was incorporated with the most ancient Laws, both Civil and Ecclesiastical, of this realm;—that it was confirmed by Statutes in the period immediately preceding the Reformation;—that it continued unaltered and unaffected during the whole of that period, and afterwards; Penitential Confession having been not only allowed, but sanctioned generally, and enjoined in some cases, by the Rubrics of the several Books of Common Prayer, and by the Book now required to be used, without any enactment in any single statute, expressly or impliedly interfering with its secrecy;—while this secrecy is expressly commanded by the Canons made since the Reformation, and declared by the Courts to be binding upon the Clergy.

Under these circumstances, I know not how any person can venture to affirm, that confessions are not privileged in Courts of Justice. Even if Sta-

tutes and Canons had left this privilege doubtful,
which I fearlessly maintain that they have not, it
exists, as we have seen, by the Common Law ; and
therefore the legal maxim would apply to it, " Quæ
Communi Legi derogant, stricte interpretari debent."* In a word, if Confession is authorized, or
permitted, as a religious Rite, its secrecy is authorized and permitted also; for without it, the Rite
itself is neutralized, and the rules which sanction it
are a dead letter ;—but, as was well said by Baron
Alderson, in another case,† " if you make a thing
lawful to be done, it is lawful in all its conse-
quences."

With respect to the policy or expediency of
allowing this privilege, it is no part of my present
undertaking to discuss it ;—my object is simply to
ascertain what the Law really is, not whether it is
good or bad. But I may be allowed to state my
firm conviction, that it is of the utmost importance,
even in a social point of view, to maintain the privilege to its full extent. There can be no doubt,
that so far from tending to defeat the administration of Justice, it aids and strengthens it in a
degree, of which probably none but those, who are
in the habit of receiving the confessions of penitents, are at all aware : but it is notorious, particu-

* Jenk. Cent. 29 ; Vin. Abr. Vol. 20, p. 14.
† Scott's Case, 1 Dears. & Bell's C. C. R. 67.

larly in Ireland, that the restitution of stolen property, and satisfaction for many other wrongs
committed, as well as the prevention of very many
crimes, are brought about by the exhortations of
the Priest in the Confessional, and by his refusal of
absolution to those who reject his salutary admo-
nitions. Look, again, to the cruelty which you
inflict on the penitent, if you cut him off from
the comfort, and the benefit, of freely and securely
unburthening his conscience, in the manner most
satisfactory to himself. What is so likely to lead
him to an entire reformation of his life, "to turn
"him from darkness to light, and from the power of
"Satan unto God," as the solemnity of Penitential
Confession, and the engagements to holiness which
he is then required to make?—and is it not, or
may it not be, as important to him, in regard to
his eternal interests, to allow him the most full and
confidential intercourse with his spiritual adviser,
as it is to his temporal, to secure to him the same
advantage in his communications with his solicitor
or his attorney?—But it is not only cruelty which
you inflict, if you practically deny him this Rite of
his religion; you act fraudulently and deceitfully towards him:— you urge him, nay, you enjoin him,
to confess his sins, if he has any which weigh
heavily upon his conscience, but you convert the

Minister to whom he resorts, into an Informer and a Spy; and while you thus deceive the penitent by hollow exhortations to his duty, and by false professions of Religion, of sanctity, and of regard for his security, you at the same time compel the Minister to act a perfidious part, and to violate his most sacred obligations, not only as a Minister of Religion, but even as a Gentleman, and a Man of honour. To require the secrets of confession to be disclosed is, to my mind, a most iniquitous and disgusting tyranny, utterly unworthy of any system of Laws which professes to be religious, or just, or humane. It cannot even be excused on the ground of public policy or expediency:—For what injury to the public can this privilege cause? Was it productive of injury, when it existed undisputed in this country in former days?—Is it found to be injurious in Scotland, where it has always prevailed?—Or in France, where the violation of it is visited with, I believe, civil, as well as ecclesiastical, punishment?—Why is it more to be dreaded here than in America, where the States of Missouri and New York, not to mention others, protect the Ministers of every religious denomination, from disclosing anything which they have learnt in confession? Why may it not be allowed here, as well as in Russia, where, under the Laws of Peter the

Great, the Seal of Confession is very strictly preserved ; and where the Emperor Nicholas, as I have been informed, once banished a Priest, who had violated it, to Siberia, although his offence was committed to serve the ends of justice ?

If other countries, not only Catholic but Protestant, find the privilege not inconsistent with the administration of justice, or with the other interests of Society, why should it be otherwise in this? Away then with the miserable pretext of policy or expediency, to which no liberal or enlightened mind can possibly resort, even if it were worth any thing, when so many considerations of far higher import, and of far nobler character, point so clearly in the opposite direction. " Summa ratio est quæ pro Religione facit," is an old maxim of English Law ;* and no person, I am satisfied, who knows anything of the subject, or considers it seriously, can reasonably doubt, that the cause of Religion is deeply interested, in maintaining the sacred inviolability of Confession.

And now I must conclude my letter. I hope that I have convinced you, that the point of law, which I have endeavoured, however feebly, to establish, is correct, or that at all events it has not yet been overruled by authority, and cannot now be

* Wingate's Max. p. 3 ; Broome's Legal Max. p. 15, &c.

set aside, either by inconsiderate assertions, or by foregone conclusions.

I am ever,

My dear Sir,

Your very faithful Servant,

EDWARD BADELEY.